WAR STORIES

SNEAKY SPIES

Charlotte Guillain

www.raintreepublishers.co.uk
Visit our website to find out
more information about
Raintree books.

To order:
☎ Phone 0845 6044371
📠 Fax +44 (0) 1865 312263
💻 Email myorders@raintreepublishers.co.uk

Customers from outside the UK please telephone +44 1865 312262

Raintree is an imprint of Capstone Global Library
Limited, a company incorporated in England and
Wales having its registered office at 7 Pilgrim Street,
London, EC4V 6LB – Registered company number:
6695582

Edited by Louise Galpine and Vaarunika Dharmapala
Designed by Clare Webber and Steve Mead
Original illustrations © Capstone Global Library
 Ltd 2011
Illustrated by KJA-Artists.com
Picture research by Elizabeth Alexander
Originated by Capstone Global Library Ltd
Printed and bound in China by Leo Paper
 Products Ltd

ISBN 978 1 406 22200 5 (hardback)
15 14 13 12 11
10 9 8 7 6 5 4 3 2 1

British Library Cataloguing in Publication Data
Guillain, Charlotte.
Sneaky spies. – (War stories)
327.1'2'09-dc22
A full catalogue record for this book is available
from the British Library.

Acknowledgements
We would like to thank the following for permission
to reproduce photographs: Alamy pp. 7 (© The
Art Gallery Collection), 16 (© The Art Archive);
Corbis pp. 6 (© Sarah Jackson; Edifice), 9 (©
Bettmann), 11 (© Bettmann), 15 (© Hulton-Deutsch
Collection), 22 (© George Steinmetz), 27 (© HO/
Reuters); Getty Images pp. 5 (Express/Hulton
Archive), 13 (Popperfoto), 14 (Central Press/
Hulton Archive), 19 (AFP), 20 (Hulton Archive), 21,
24 (CNN); Shutterstock p. 17 (© Fedor Selivanov),
background design and features (© oriontrail);
Virginia Historical Society p. 10.

Cover photograph of the shadows of two men
with briefcase shaking hands reproduced with
permission of Getty Images (Julian Hibbard/
Photonica).

We would like to thank John Allen Williams for his
invaluable help in the preparation of this book.

Every effort has been made to contact copyright
holders of material reproduced in this book. Any
omissions will be rectified in subsequent printings
if notice is given to the publisher.

CONTENTS

Words appearing in the text in bold, **like this**, are explained in the glossary.

Look out for these boxes:

WHAT WOULD YOU DO?
Imagine what it would be like to make difficult choices in wartime.

REMEMBERING BRAVERY
Find out about the ways in which we remember courageous acts today.

NUMBER CRUNCHING
Learn the facts and figures about wars and battles.

SECRET HEROES
Find out about the brave individuals who didn't make it into the history books.

Spying on another country or army is called **espionage**. Espionage has been used in wars and during peacetime throughout history. Rulers sent their spies on missions to gather secret information about other powers. This information could help a ruler or **military** leader to work out what an enemy was planning to do. Countries also used spies to spread false information to trick their enemies.

Risk takers

Spies in the past had to be skilled in disguising and hiding themselves. They took great risks moving behind enemy lines and faced terrible punishment if they were caught. Throughout history both women and men have worked as spies. Their work could help decide who won a war.

Today, espionage often uses technology rather than people. Satellites and electronic devices can be used to gather information without putting spies at so much risk. However, spies do still operate today in some countries.

This book will look at how espionage has changed over the years. It will show how some of the skills used by spies thousands of years ago are still effective today.

REMEMBERING BRAVERY

Many people are fascinated by the secret world of spies. Books and films about espionage have always been popular. They often tell the stories of brave spies who worked in dangerous situations to get any information that could help their country.

▲ The author Ian Fleming created one of the most
famous fictional spies, James Bond. Ian Fleming
fought with the British Royal Navy in World War II.

THE FIRST SPIES

Rulers and **military** leaders have used spies for thousands of years. Around 1274 BC, the ancient Egyptians were at war with the Hittite **Empire** in the Middle East. Egypt's ruler, Pharaoh Rameses II, wanted more land. As his army approached the city of Kadesh, Hittite spies met him. They gave the Egyptians false information about the Hittite army's location. Rameses nearly fell into the trap but when he captured two other spies he forced them to tell the truth.

WHAT WOULD YOU DO?

Rameses II had the two Hittite spies beaten so they would give him accurate information. What would you have done? Do you think beating or torturing spies is an acceptable way to get **intelligence**?

► Rameses II was known as Rameses the Great because he was one of the most powerful and skilful rulers of Ancient Egypt.

Spymaster

Sun Tzu was a military general who lived in ancient China during the Zhou dynasty (around 1050–256 BC). He wrote a book called *The Art of War* explaining that a good way to beat an enemy was to gain knowledge about them. He identified five different types of spy:

- local spies – ordinary people living among the enemy

- internal spies – the enemy's **officials**

- double spies – the enemy's spies

- dead spies – **agents** who are given false information to spread to the enemy

- living spies – agents who return from the enemy with a report.

Sun Tzu also wrote about how important it was to keep **espionage** secret!

► Sun Tzu's ideas about espionage have been used in wars throughout history and all around the world.

The American Civil War

The American **Civil War** (1861–1865) was fought between the **Confederates** and the **Union** in the United States. The Confederates were 11 southern states who wanted to break away from the rest of the country. The two sides also fought over other issues, such as slavery.

▼ This map shows which states belonged to the Union and Confederate sides in the American Civil War.

Union spymasters

Both sides used spies to gather information about the enemy. Allan Pinkerton was a key figure in Union espionage. He worked closely with President Abraham Lincoln to ensure his safety, and set up a network of spies for Major General McClellan, one of the generals of the Union army.

Pinkerton's agents introduced espionage techniques such as working undercover. He even went on undercover missions himself, working among the Confederates and sending intelligence back to McClellan. Meanwhile, another Union spymaster, Lafayette Baker, and his agents sent information to another Union general. The two spymasters worked so secretly they even kept information from each other!

▲ Here you can see President Abraham Lincoln (centre), Major General McClellan (right), and Allan Pinkerton.

NUMBER CRUNCHING

The table below shows roughly how many soldiers and sailors historians believe died during the American Civil War. In addition, as many as 620,000 **civilians** may have died.

Army	Deaths in battle	Deaths from disease, malnutrition, and extreme weather	Total number of military deaths
Union	110,000	250,000	360,000
Confederate	94,000	164,000	258,000

Union spies

Elizabeth Van Lew worked as a Union spy. She visited Union prisoners of war and gave them food and clothing. In return, they would give her useful military information, which she would pass on to generals from the Union army.

George Curtis worked disguised as a merchant, selling illegal goods from the north to the Confederates. He gathered intelligence as he travelled. John Scobell was an escaped slave who worked for Pinkerton. He was skilled at changing his identity and often pretended to be a servant. He discovered important information about Confederate supplies and plans.

◀ This is the Union spy Elizabeth Van Lew.

Confederate spies

One of the most famous Confederate spies was Belle Boyd. She persuaded Union soldiers to reveal military secrets, and once hid in a cupboard to overhear a Union general briefing his staff. She risked her own life, and that of her slave, delivering information to the Confederates.

Rose O'Neal Greenhow managed to send intelligence to the Confederates from prison. She did this by burning a certain number of candles in her window or by hiding messages in visitors' hair.

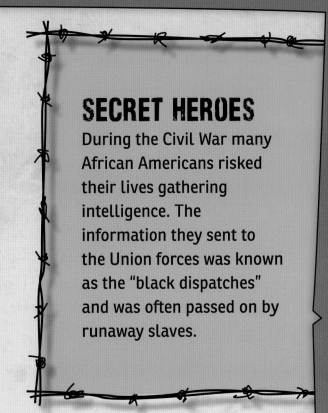

SECRET HEROES

During the Civil War many African Americans risked their lives gathering intelligence. The information they sent to the Union forces was known as the "black dispatches" and was often passed on by runaway slaves.

◄ Belle Boyd became a spy when Union soldiers took down her Confederate flag and were rude to her mother! She shot a Union soldier and from then on worked as a spy.

ESPIONAGE DURING WORLD WAR I AND II

In the first half of the 20th century there were two world wars. World War I took place from 1914 to 1918. Germany wanted to increase the size of its **empire**. Soldiers from the United Kingdom, the United States, France, Russia, Australia, India, and many other countries fought in terrible battles against Germany and its supporters. Both sides used **espionage** to gain **intelligence** to help them win the war.

▲ This map shows you which European countries fought with Germany (the Central Powers) and which fought with the United Kingdom and the United States (the Allies).

Mata Hari

Mata Hari was a Dutch dancer living in Paris. Her real name was Margaretha Zelle. During the war she often travelled and met **military** officers from both sides. Mata Hari claimed she tricked the Germans into thinking she was working for them when she was really spying for France. But the French did not trust her. In 1917 they executed her for being a **double agent** working for Germany. It was later revealed that she was innocent and a real double agent may have lied about her.

German agent

During World War I several German **agents** were caught spying in Britain. Carl Hans Lody was sent to spy on the Royal Navy in Scotland, gathering intelligence about ships, weapons, and the damage caused by battles. Unfortunately, he had not been trained as a spy and he sent telegrams without using **code**. The British **intercepted** his messages and only sent the ones that contained incorrect information on to Germany. He was eventually arrested and executed.

▶ This is the German spy Carl Hans Lody.

World War II

After World War I, Germany was weak. As leader of the country, Adolf Hitler was popular for making Germany strong again. He made **alliances** with Italy and Japan and these countries began invading other countries. This led to World War II (1939–1945). Spies played an important role, gathering intelligence and tricking the enemy.

The White Rabbit

Edward Yeo-Thomas was a British agent whose codename was "the White Rabbit". During World War II he helped to organize the French Resistance against the **Nazis**. He was at constant risk of being discovered. Once he even hid from the Germans in a hearse (a car used for funerals). He was finally captured and tortured. He was sent to a prison camp but he survived the war.

REMEMBERING BRAVERY

Edward Yeo-Thomas risked his life many times. His work was remembered in books and a film, *The White Rabbit*. There is also a plaque outside his house in London describing his brave work during World War II.

Agent GARBO

Juan Pujol, whose code name was GARBO, wanted to spy for the British but they turned him down. He went ahead anyway and approached the Germans. He worked as a double agent, making the Germans think he was working for them, while supplying intelligence to Britain. He also gave the Germans false information about agents working in Britain. None of them existed! Eventually the British realized how useful he was and his work helped defeat the Germans.

▼ Juan Pujol fought in the Spanish **Civil War** (1936–1939). He fought on the opposite side to these soldiers, who were supported by Nazi Germany. Pujol said his experiences fighting against men like these made him want to contribute to "the good of humanity".

Spies in America

The United States did not join the war until 1941, but spies were sent there to gather intelligence before this date. A group of German spies called the Duquesne spy ring worked in key jobs to gather information that could be used if the United States joined the war. Some worked for delivery services, sending secret messages alongside the proper mail. The double agent William Sebold helped the Americans to identify and arrest the spies.

NUMBER CRUNCHING

During World War II people worried that foreigners living in their country were spies working for the enemy. Many of these people were imprisoned in camps until the end of the war. Thousands of Germans, Austrians, and Italians were imprisoned in the United Kingdom, including Jews. In 1940 more than 7,500 internees were sent to Canada and Australia from the United Kingdom.

▼ Foreigners in the United States were imprisoned, too. These Japanese Americans are about to be transported to an **internment camp**. Even children were interned.

Mary Bancroft

Mary Bancroft was an American spy during World War II. She lived in Switzerland, and could speak French and German. She was also good at getting people to trust her. She worked with Germans who were against the Nazis, passing on information from them and **translating** German documents for US intelligence services. She had to be sure that the people she worked with were not double agents who were trying to trick her. This took a lot of skill and courage.

▲ Mary Bancroft lived and carried out her espionage in Switzerland.

SPIES OF THE COLD WAR

After World War II **espionage** was still important. This period was known as the **Cold War** (1947–1991), when there was tension between countries such as the **Soviet Union** and the United States, western Europe, and their supporters. Both sides were very worried about the other developing and using nuclear weapons against them.

Who was spying?

The Soviet Union and the countries allied to it were **communist**. Many spies working for them in the West agreed with these political beliefs. The West had its own network of spies gathering **intelligence** on the communist enemy. This was a very suspicious time, with countries such as East Germany using spies to watch their own people.

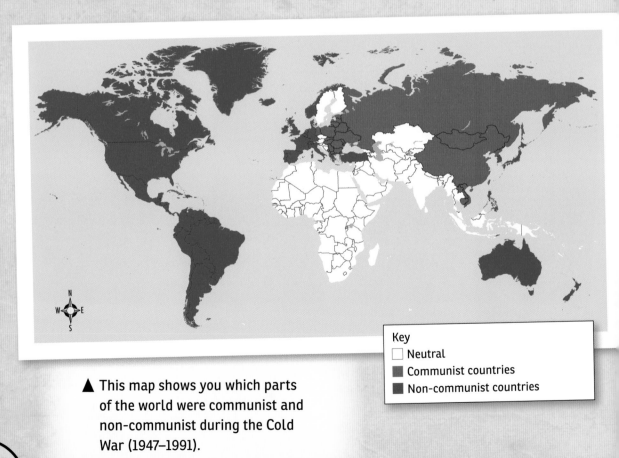

Key
▢ Neutral
◼ Communist countries
◼ Non-communist countries

▲ This map shows you which parts of the world were communist and non-communist during the Cold War (1947–1991).

Soviet spies

The Soviet Union **recruited** spies in the United States and western Europe. Often these **agents** were scientists with access to information about nuclear weapons. Klaus Fuchs passed on information that helped the Soviets with their own weapons development. He was discovered and arrested in 1950. Then other spies were arrested, including husband and wife Julius and Ethel Rosenberg in the United States. The Rosenbergs were executed. Although many people now think Ethel was innocent, others also believe she at least knew of her husband's activities.

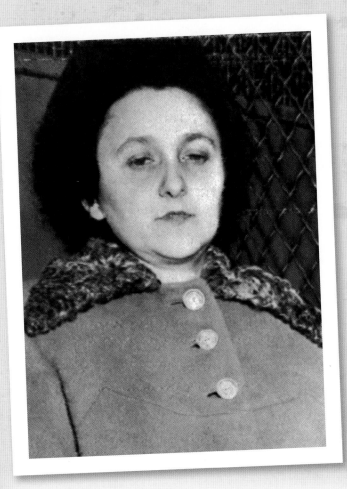

WHAT WOULD YOU DO?

Many spies were put in a difficult position, often having to choose between their beliefs and their country, family, and friends. Others were blackmailed and forced to spy. What would you have done if you were asked to spy on your own friends and family?

▲ This photograph shows Ethel Rosenberg. It was said that Ethel typed up the secrets her husband wanted to send to the Soviet Union.

The Cambridge Spies

The Cambridge Spies were a group of five British communists who studied at Cambridge University in the 1930s. The Soviets recruited the five students in the hope they would eventually have important jobs and share useful intelligence. By the start of World War II, this had happened. Kim Philby, Guy Burgess, Donald Maclean, and Anthony Blunt all had important jobs and contacts in government and the secret service. They passed secrets to the Soviets until the 1950s.

▲ Here you can see Anthony Blunt (far left), Donald Maclean (centre), Kim Philby (right), and Guy Burgess (bottom).

SECRET HEROES

It is thought that the fifth member of the spy ring was John Cairncross, who was exposed in 1951. Do you think he was a hero for spying because of his beliefs, or was he a traitor to his country?

Suspicions

However, the Soviets were deeply suspicious of the spies. They worried that the five might be **double agents** passing secrets back to the British. Eventually the British started to track the spy ring down. Burgess and Maclean disappeared in 1951 and fled to the Soviet Union. Philby managed to convince the authorities that he was innocent but eventually **defected** in 1963. Blunt secretly confessed to being a spy in 1964, sharing intelligence about the Soviets in return for his freedom.

▲ Gary Powers was an American spy plane pilot who was shot down over Soviet airspace in 1960. He served two years in jail and then was swapped for a Soviet spy who had been captured in the West.

TECHNOLOGY AND MODERN WARS

Espionage has changed a lot. Today, technology plays a large part in the gathering of **intelligence**. **Agents** can monitor activity on the internet to gather information about individuals or groups that threaten security. Satellites and unmanned spy planes take photographs from the air to help governments keep an eye on other countries or terrorists. Technology has changed the way spies share their information. Even so, in many ways spies continue to work in the same way they have for thousands of years.

▼ The cameras on the bottom of this MQ-Predator spy plane can record clear pictures of the ground, even in the dark.

Spy HQ

The British Security Service (MI5) gathers secret intelligence in a number of ways. Some of these methods are ancient and others use the most modern technology. The main ways MI5 gets information are:

- **covert** human intelligence sources – agents who are not part of MI5 providing reports

- directed surveillance – watching and tracking possible enemies

- **interception** of communication – keeping an eye on emails and other electronic communication

- intrusive surveillance – using special devices to bug a house or car and listen to conversations and activities.

The Secret Intelligence Service (MI6) gathers intelligence abroad.

NUMBER CRUNCHING

The MQ-Predator is an unmanned spy plane that is often used by the United States Air Force. A pilot controls the plane from the ground while an intelligence co-ordinator looks at the video that is sent from the plane's cameras.

Wingspan: 16.8 metres (55.11 feet)
Length: 8.22 metres (27 feet)
Top speed: 217 kph (135 mph)
Cost: $20 million (£12.75 million) (for four aircraft, ground control stations, and satellite link).

Hacking Hanssen

In 2001, Robert Hanssen was arrested in Virginia, USA. He worked for the Federal Bureau of Investigation (FBI). This agency gathers intelligence that might affect the national security of the United States. For 22 years, Robert Hanssen had sold US secrets to Russia for large amounts of money. When his wife became suspicious, he told her that he had been passing on false information to the Russians as part of his job. Hanssen was skilled at using computers and could hack into other FBI agents' files for information. He was finally recognized on a tape given to the FBI by a Russian spy and put in prison for life.

Emailed secrets

In 2009, a Russian called Gennady Sipachev was sent to prison for passing secrets to the United States. He had emailed secret **military** maps giving information about Russian forces nearly 20 years after the **Cold War** had finished. Most people think he passed on these secrets to the United States for money, like Hanssen. The espionage was embarrassing for both sides because the two nations were supposed to be friendly.

NUMBER CRUNCHING

The US Central Intelligence Agency (CIA) gathers information on 266 nations. This information is online in the *World Factbook* at www.cia.gov/library/publications/the-world-factbook/index.html.

One of the world's most recent wars has been fought in Afghanistan. Here is some information on Afghanistan from the *World Factbook*:

Area: 652,230 kilometres^2 (251,827 miles^2)
Population: 29,121,286
Life expectancy for men: 44.45 years
Life expectancy for women: 44.87 years

◀ Robert Hanssen, seen here on blurry video footage being arrested by FBI agents, sold secrets for money and diamonds, not for his political beliefs.

CONCLUSION

Espionage has been used for thousands of years. Whenever nations have not trusted each other, they have used spies to try to get an advantage. Sun Tzu's opinions on the ways spies can work are still relevant today. The modern world is very different and technology has affected the way in which spies gather and share information, but the basics of espionage remain the same. Spies continue to gather **intelligence** that will give their side an advantage and mislead the enemy.

Intelligence

Today, armies gather information and try to trick the enemy in much the same way that ancient generals and spies did. **Military** personnel try to guess the enemy's plans. They also try to stop the enemy from guessing what their fellow soldiers are planning. This can be dangerous work, often performed close to the enemy and ahead of other troops.

REMEMBERING BRAVERY

The first British woman to be killed in the war in Afghanistan was Corporal Sarah Bryant, in 2008. She worked in the British Army Intelligence Corps. Like other soldiers killed in Afghanistan, her friends and family have remembered her on special websites. The army also has a memorial garden where the names of the dead are recorded on a monument.

▼ This satellite photograph shows a nuclear fuel facility in Iran. Spy satellites are often used in modern espionage.

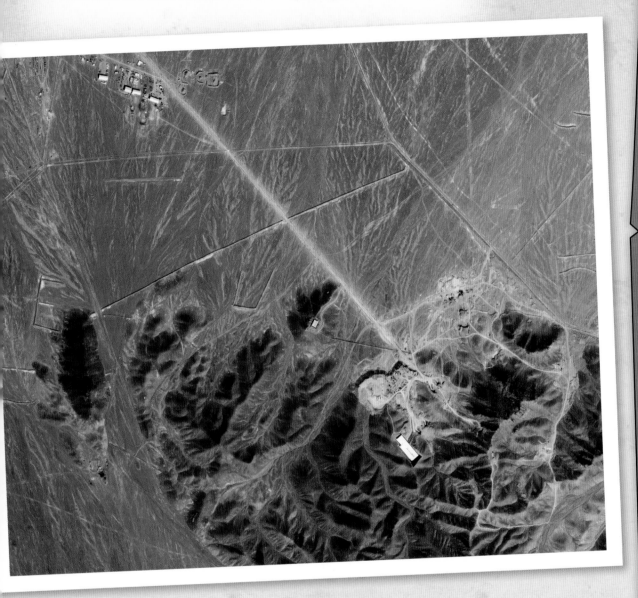

Future spies

Perhaps espionage in the future will rely more and more on technology and spies will not find themselves in dangerous situations in the field. Or perhaps spies will only ever be able to gather useful intelligence by getting close to the enemy. What do you think?

SNEAKY SPIES AROUND THE WORLD

USA

American spies were at work during the **Civil War** and **espionage** has continued in the USA ever since. Julius Rosenberg and Robert Hanssen spied in the USA.

N
W E
S

UNITED KINGDOM
During World War I and World War II German spies came to the United Kingdom to gather intelligence. The Cambridge spies were also **recruited** in the UK.

SOVIET UNION
Julius Rosenberg, Klaus Fuchs, the Cambridge Spies, and Robert Hanssen all spied for the **Soviet Union**.

CHINA
Sun Tzu, a military general in ancient China, wrote *The Art of War*. His book has been used as a guide to espionage for centuries.

GERMANY
Carl Hans Lody spied for Germany during World War I. The Duquesne spy ring working in the United States during World War II also worked for Germany.

AFGHANISTAN
Today, forces in Afghanistan gather intelligence using unmanned spy planes.

EGYPT
Ancient Egyptian ruler Pharaoh Rameses II captured enemy spies and had them beaten so that they would reveal secret information.

SPAIN
Juan Pujol wanted to spy against Germany because he hated the **Nazis** after their involvement in the Spanish Civil War (1936–1939).

GLOSSARY

agent person acting on the orders of an organization or country

alliance union of two or more sides

civil war war between different groups of people within the same country

civilian ordinary person who is not part of the military

code letters, numbers, or signs used to send secret messages

Cold War period from the end of World War II to the break-up of the Soviet Union when the United States and its supporters prepared for war against the Soviet Union

communist system of government where one party controls what goods are produced in a country

Confederate one of the southern states in the United States that wanted to break away and form their own government in the 1800s

covert actions that are secret

defect desert your country for political reasons

double agent spy who works for one side while pretending to work for the other

empire large number of countries ruled by one country

espionage act of spying

intelligence information gathered by spies

intercept interrupt and look at information, usually unknown to the sender and recipient

internment camp place where people are confined, usually during war

military to do with the armed forces

Nazi ruling party of Germany from 1933 to 1945, or a member of it. The Nazis were led by Adolf Hitler.

official person holding a position within an organization

recruit enlist people to serve an organization, group, or country

Soviet Union former communist state made up of Russia and several neighbouring countries. The Soviet Union existed between 1922 and 1991.

translate express the meaning of something in another language

Union states that made up the United States after some southern states tried to set up their own government in the 1800s

FIND OUT MORE

Books

Kingfisher Knowledge: Spies, Clive Gifford (Kingfisher, 2007)

Spies and Spying: Wartime Spies, Andrew Langley (Franklin Watts, 2009)

Spies!: Real People, Real Stories, Laura Portalupi (Red Brick Learning, 2005)

Websites

www.mi5.gov.uk/output/mi5-history-for-schools.html
The official website for MI5, the British Security Service, has a history section with lots of information on espionage.

www.mi6.gov.uk/output/sis-home-welcome.html
MI6, the British Secret Intelligence Service, has a history and records section on its website.

https://www.cia.gov/kids-page/index.html
Learn more about the CIA on their website. There are also lots of games to play and puzzles to solve.

Places to visit

The Imperial War Museum
Lambeth Road
London
SE1 6HZ
www.iwm.org.uk

The British Museum
Great Russell Street
London
WC1B 3DG
www.britishmuseum.org

Visit the Imperial War Museum and the British Museum to learn more about the wars and countries discussed in this book.

INDEX